the ESTELLE LIEBLING

vocal course

for
BARITONE
BASS BARITONE
and
BASS (BASSO)

edited by bernard whitefield

chappell music company

FOREWORD

The voice is at one and the same time the simplest and the most difficult of all musical instruments to play. It is the "simplest" because nature endowed each of us with a voice — it is part of our normal equipment and, as such, it is made to work automatically. It is also the most difficult because the vocal mechanism is within the body — it is invisible. The piano student, for instance, can observe the workings of his fingers on the keyboard, and he can listen to the quality of tone he produces thereby. But the vocal student cannot watch his vocal apparatus at all. It takes study and a singing instinct to learn to listen critically to your own voice. FOR THESE REASONS ALONE, THE VOCAL STUDENT CANNOT HOPE TO LEARN TO SING WELL WITHOUT A GOOD VOICE TEACHER.

We must realize that all methods have the same goal — beautiful singing. But all voices cannot be taught in the same way. We teachers must be prepared to adapt and re-adapt our methods twenty-five times a day, if twenty-five different pupils appear before us. Every one of those pupils must be taught from the standpoint of the individual, taking into consideration his mental, temperamental, musical and educational background. Sometimes we may find it necessary to make up with technique and resourcefulness what may be lacking in quality. But it should be remembered that all voices can be ENHANCED BY PURE INTONATION, CHARM OF LINE, SUBTLETY OF INTERPRETATION AND METICULOUS ATTENTION TO DICTION.

Each of these books consists of three parts: PART I describes the vocal mechanism and its functions briefly and in simple, non-technical language. A general knowledge of the instrument often helps the student to clarify a question of tone production. PART II, forming the major portion of the book, consists of basic, fundamental vocalises carefully selected to develop the specific voices for which the book is written. PART III presents the important elements of diction in the five languages most commonly used in singing: English, Italian, French, German and Spanish.

BEL CANTO is an Italian term which has no other meaning than its literal translation — BEAUTIFUL SINGING. And knowledge of beautiful singing today is based on four centuries of experiment and intense study on the part of many great teachers and singers. There is nothing mysterious, mystical or mythical about it! Assuming that the student has a good natural voice and talent, there is no reason why he or she may not become a fine singer, given the proper training. The student must realize, however, that there are no short cuts to becoming an artist any more than to becoming successful in any other profession: The surgeon must also study medicine, the architect must also have a sound knowledge of engineering principles. So, in order to enter the musical profession, you must not only learn the technique of singing, but — and this is the most important thing of all — YOU MUST STUDY MUSIC!

Now a final word as to the requirements for the various branches of the vocal profession. Regardless of the field in which the student will eventually specialize, technique and musicianship will be invaluable. This is not only true for opera, concert and oratorio, but also in the fields of popular singing. Although the so-called "serious" branches of singing generally require a voice of greater range and power, nevertheless the chief difference between "serious" and "popular" singing is a matter mainly of style. Even in those exceptional cases where style may be instinctive, it is enhanced by a sound technique and musical knowledge. For "knowing how" is the key to expressing what you want to say in a song, with the proper style!

THIS SERIES OF BOOKS IS DEVOTED TO THE EXPOSITION OF THE FUNDAMENTALS OF VOICE CULTURE, A SUBJECT WHICH HAS BEEN MY PRIME CONCERN DURING MANY YEARS OF SINGING AND TEACHING. IT IS FOR MY FELLOW TEACHERS THAT I AM DETAILING WHAT I HAVE OBSERVED, LEARNED AND EXPERIENCED IN THE COURSE OF MY PROFESSION, AND I DEDICATE THESE BOOKS TO MY COLLEAGUES WITH MY REGARD AND RESPECT.

ESTELLE LIEBLING

CONTENTS

PART I — THE VOCAL MECHANISM

PART II — VOCAL STUDIES

PART III — DICTION

PART I — THE VOCAL MECHANISM

The process of singing involves four main systems of the body which together form the vocal mechanism: 1 — The BREATH system, which provides the motivating force. 2 — The PHONATING system, which produces the tones. 3 — The RESO-NATING system, which reinforces and beautifies the tone. 4 — The ARTICULATING system, which forms the vowels and consonants of the words we sing.

THE BREATH SYSTEM

The functions of the breathing apparatus will be more easily grasped if we break it down into three parts: BREATHING, POSTURE and BREATH CONTROL.

Breathing

1 — Normally, breathing serves the purpose of supplying us with life-giving oxygen and carrying off waste matter. The act of breathing, called RESPIRATION, consists of two parts: inspiration or inhaling, and expiration or exhaling. In short, breathing IN and breathing OUT.

2 — Ordinarily, the amount of air which we respire is automatically governed by our needs:—

   A — When we sit quietly, we need very little oxygen and we breathe calmly, the air going in and out through the nose slowly.

   B — But if we run, for example, we need great amounts of oxygen and we quickly take in and expel large quantities of air through the open mouth.

3 — In singing, however, we must combine A and B in different ways:

   I — We breathe in and out through the MOUTH practically always.

   II — We INHALE a comparatively LARGE quantity of air QUICKLY.

   III — We EXHALE a comparatively SMALL quantity of air SLOWLY.

(Breathing through the nose is relaxing and restful. But it can only be done in singing during fairly long rests in the music and should be the exception and not the rule. However, taking advantage of such rests, we find that a combination of mouth and nose breathing is an ideal method.)

Posture

But in order to breathe properly we must have GOOD POSTURE.

The quickest way to find correct posture is to stand with your back against a wall: The BACKS of the heels, hips, shoulders, and head should firmly touch the wall. The head should be held so that the eyes may naturally look straight ahead. (Use the wall only to verify or correct your posture. Once you have it, step away from the wall without changing your posture.) Remember: CHEST OUT, SHOULDERS DOWN, STOMACH IN. With correct posture you are in a position to achieve breath control.

Breath Control

Breath control means:—

1 — Knowing how much breath to take in (simply: a short breath for a short phrase, a long breath for a long phrase).

2 — Knowing how to inhale deeply.

3 — Knowing how to CONTROL the amount of breath you exhale.

The first statement is easy to comprehend and will be taken up later with the appropriate vocal exercises. The next two points deserve separate discussion.

But first, let us see what happens when we just breathe normally. If you were to lie flat on your back and breathe quietly, you would notice that the soft frontal area below the breast bone and the lower ribs swell out a little as you inhale. This shows us two important things:—

1 — The BOTTOM of the lungs (the largest part of those organs) INFLATE the MOST.

2 — The parts of the torso around the bottom of the lungs are MOVABLE and can STRETCH OUTWARD.

It is clear then that this is the way nature meant us to breathe, and to use any other method would be incorrect. Let us keep this in mind as we continue.

The breath system itself consists of the following parts:—

1 — The chest.

2 — The lungs.

3 — The diaphragm — a sheet of muscle shaped like the crown of a man's Homburg hat. It extends horizontally all around the inside of the lower chest and separates the heart and lungs from the lower organs.

4 — The lower ribs, which are movable.

5 — The muscles all around the lower part of the chest and the upper part of the abdomen. The upper abdomen, which extends around the FRONT of the body between the lowest ribs and the tops of the hip bones, must be FLEXIBLE.

Singing is often referred to as SUSTAINED SPEECH. Obviously, to sustain, or hold, a singing tone we need more breath than for a short spoken tone. And we must realize that the vocal chords produce tone when they are set in vibration by BREATH PRESSURE. Now let us see how this pressure is created.

Breath Control — Inhaling

When we take a deep breath in order to sing, the breath system acts as follows:—

1 — The chest, which is held high in good posture, must be MOTIONLESS.

2 — The diaphragm FLATTENS DOWN and OUTWARD. As a result, the next steps occur automatically.

3 — The lower organs are pushed down and in turn cause the abdomen to distend a bit (push forward).

4 — The lower ribs are pushed OUTWARD ALL AROUND THE BODY.

5 — These movements create a large "empty" space which is naturally filled by the bottom of the inflated lungs.

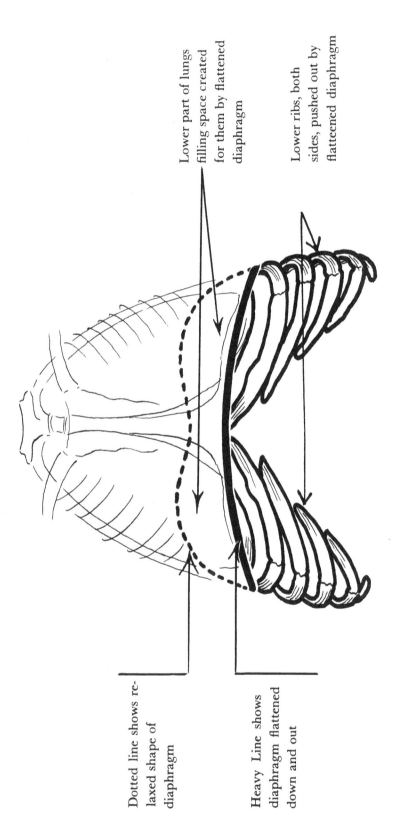

Lower part of lungs
filling space created
for them by flattened
diaphragm

Lower ribs, both
sides, pushed out by
flatteened diaphragm

Dotted line shows re-
laxed shape of
diaphragm

Heavy Line shows
diaphragm flattened
down and out

FRONT VIEW OF DEEP BREATH

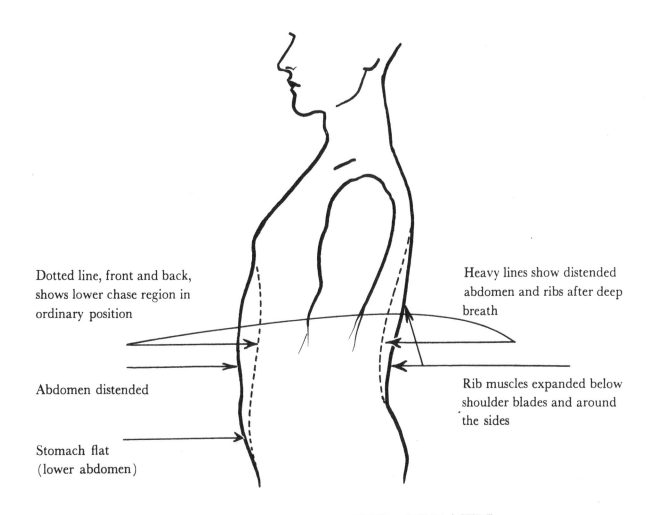

Dotted line, front and back, shows lower chase region in ordinary position

Heavy lines show distended abdomen and ribs after deep breath

Abdomen distended

Rib muscles expanded below shoulder blades and around the sides

Stomach flat (lower abdomen)

SIDE VIEW OF DEEP BREATH

Breath Control — Exhaling

Now that you have taken a deep breath properly, you must learn how to expel it as SLOWLY and STEADILY as possible. In other words, you must CONTROL the amount of breath you emit. Remember, when singing a song you must sing a group of notes on one breath, because the notes carry a group of words and the word-group conveys a thought. This is known as a PHRASE. If you breathe in the middle of most phrases you will spoil both the flow of the melody and the meaning of the words. Also, try to finish each phrase with a little breath left over. It is not artistic to end a phrase feeling that you have barely managed to get there.

The act of expelling the breath is controlled by the DIAPHRAGM and the MUSCLES of the LOWER RIBS and ABDOMEN. They operate as follows:—

1 — Those muscles SLOWLY and GRADUALLY exert pressure inwards.

2 — As they do so they create pressure on the air in the lungs.

3 — This causes the air to pass up and out through the throat which contains the vocal chords.

4 — The vocal chords, as we shall see later, automatically shape themselves for the tone you want. And the breath pressure sets them in vibration.

5 — While exhaling, the chest NEVER sinks down. For if it did, your breath system would collapse and you could not support the tone.

It cannot be emphasized strongly enough that the tone must be SUPPORTED by controlled breath. We repeat: SUPPORT THE TONE.

Breath Control Exercise

The amount of breath you must inhale is decided by the length of the phrase you must sing: a short breath for a short phrase, a long breath for a long phrase. If you have more breath than you need, you place an unnecessary strain on your breathing muscles and run the risk of making the tones breathy.

But in the beginning you must strengthen the breath system, and for that purpose you must learn to control long breaths. To make sure that your chest does NOT collapse practise this exercise before a mirror.

1 — Stand with CORRECT POSTURE.

2 — Breathe in deeply and both feel and watch the ABDOMEN (not the stomach) and the LOWER RIBS EXPAND.

3 — Speak the ALPHABET moderately quickly as many times as you can on ONE BREATH.

4 — When you come to the end of your breath, do NOT allow the chest to sink down, but immediately take another deep breath and repeat the exercise.

5 — The exercise should be repeated three times in succession by the beginner.

This exercise should be done every morning. The average beginner is able to repeat the alphabet only about two or two and a half times in one breath. But after a few weeks the student will be able to do eight alphabets in one breath.

(There are two schools of thought concerning exhalation for singing, that is, controlling the outgoing breath. One side maintains that the lower ribs and abdomen should not move inward, but should remain expanded throughout the exhaling act. On the other hand, the other school advocates the controlled inward pressure of the movable ribs and abdomen, as we describe and teach it in this vocal course. The concensus of opinion of a majority of the outstanding singers and teachers favors this latter method, although many good vocalists and instructors use the former. However, in the final analysis it must be realized that both methods aim to maintain the proper amount of breath pressure for the support of good tone.)

THE PHONATING SYSTEM

Most young singers are not aware that the vocal chords can accomplish only a few things:—

1 — Produce a tone.

2 — Give a tone a certain pitch.

3 — Produce tones in different registers.

The endless variety of tone color, the whole range of emotional expression, lies in the use of other organs. These have to be trained with the same careful attention that we bestow upon the training of the vocal chords.

To help form a clear picture of the phonating, or sound, system and its functions, we outline it under three headings: the VOCAL CHORDS, the LARYNX and the REGISTERS.

The Vocal Chords

The top of the windpipe, or TRACHEA, ends in a tube shaped like a wedge. This is the LARYNX. One edge is in the front of the throat and forms the Adam's Apple in men. Imagine the inside of the larynx closed by a round sheet of muscle like a drum head. Then imagine that circle cut right down the middle from front to back. The two straight edges at the middle form the actual VOCAL CHORDS, or vocal bands. The slit between them is called the GLOTTIS.

The vocal bands are only about one-half inch long in men and a bit shorter in women. In spite of their small size they are quite strong, for nature intends them to give us a life-time of good service as the most important means of communication among people — SPEECH. But the vocal bands must not be abused; these tiny muscles cannot be treated like your large arm muscles, for instance. And bad vocal production can injure them very quickly and even ruin them. Obviously this applies to public speakers and actors as well as to singers.

When the vocal chords are not in use, the slit between them, the glottis, is wide open to allow the breath to pass in and out freely. But when we sing, this occurs:—

1 — The vocal chords are brought close together by various controlling muscles and shaped for the tone you want.

2 — That shape acts as a valve which helps automatically to decide the proper air pressure needed for that tone.

3 — As the breath pressure is applied to the shaped vocal chords they vibrate and thus the tone phonates, or sounds.

THE MOST REMARKABLE THING ABOUT THE ENTIRE PHONATING ACTION IS THAT IT TAKES PLACE AUTOMATICALLY. THE SINGER DOES NOT IN ANY WAY MANIPULATE THE VOCAL CHORDS.

To produce a fine tone the student need only:—

1 — LISTEN CAREFULLY TO THE NOTE THE TEACHER STRIKES ON THE PIANO.

2 — FORM A CLEAR MENTAL PICTURE OF THAT SOUND, that is, THINK THE TONE YOU WILL SING.

3 — KEEP GOOD POSTURE.

4 -- MAINTAIN THE PROPER BREATH SUPPORT. NOW SING.

The Larynx

The larynx is constructed mainly of muscles and cartilages which automatically adjust themselves to the action of the vocal chords. The larynx is held in position by muscles from above and below. The lower muscles are connected to the chest. Therefore, if the posture is bad, the larynx will not be able to adjust properly and the tone will be bad.

The upper muscles holding the larynx in position are attached to the tongue and to the lower jaw. Therefore, the best results when practising will be achieved if the student will stand still, not move the head about too much and maintain a pleasant expression.

Of course, when the student has become well trained, the vocal apparatus will be under such fine control that he will be able to move in any direction on a stage and still produce beautiful tones. And the facial expressions will change as a result of the mental and emotional reactions to the meaning of the words that are interpreted.

Thus we see that the only parts of the singer's body that work hard are the BRAIN and the BREATH SYSTEM. The tone producing system works AUTOMATICALLY and must be RELAXED. But remember that relaxation does not mean flabbiness. We are not rag dolls. We must maintain what the instrumentalist calls CONTROLLED RELAXATION.

(As the vocalist sings high and low the larynx will slightly rise and fall with the pitch. Obviously this requires a relaxed throat. But this action is AUTOMATIC and no attempt should be made to manipulate the larynx.)

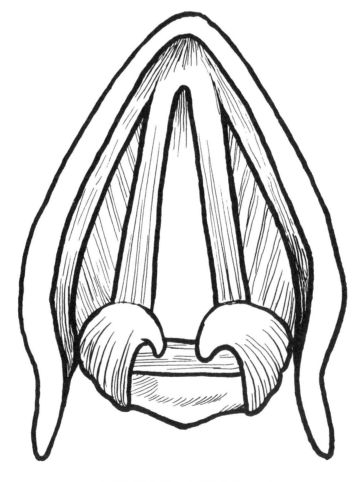

VOCAL CHORDS

The Registers

The vocal mechanism produces tones under several different automatic muscular adjustments. These are known as REGISTERS and these have long been a subject of controversy. The concensus of opinion of the best singers and teachers is that there are three registers called CHEST, MEDIUM and HEAD. However — and this is important — they do not function equally in all the voice types. The registers function as follows in the MALE voices:—

1 — If you will glance at the strings of a grand piano you will see that the lowest tones have the longest strings. In the singer's CHEST register, which produces the lowest tones, the vocal chords seem to vibrate in their full length. (The narrow slit, or glottis, between the vocal bands is opened all the way, from front to back.) The vocal vibrations are felt mainly in the chest.

2 — The medium tones of the piano are obviously played on strings of medium length. In the singer's MEDIUM register the vocal chords seem to be shortened, for they are closed a bit at both ends. This makes the glottis, the vibrating space, shorter. The vocal vibrations are felt mainly in the front of the face.

In the male voices the chest and medium registers form one long, unbroken line. The transition between these registers is entirely automatic and the singer himself is completely unaware of it . . . However, there is a point in the upper part of the medium register where an adjustment does take place in the male voice and, from there upwards, the tones must be covered. With proper training this presents no difficulties. (See THE COVERED TONE, page 23.)

3 — A final glance at the piano shows that the strings for the highest tones are the shortest. Thus, in the singer's HEAD register the vocal chords seem to be used in only about half their length, both ends being closed. But the front end is closed to greater extent than the back end. The glottis is thereby moved a bit to the rear. In the head register the voice seems to float up through the top of the head.

The head register in male singers is not a "regular" part of the male voice as it is in the female voice. The reason is that in the male voice the pure head tones have an entirely different quality from those in his lower registers and furthermore, they are quite weak and have little carrying power. Because of this there are two schools of opinion as to the value of developing this register in the male voice. While one school of eminent teachers and singers prefers to disregard it, the other school considers it of some importance for certain purposes. For these reasons we shall discuss the subject pro and con briefly and leave it to the teacher to use his or her own judgment in the matter (see THE HEAD VOICE, page 44).

In short, a "register" refers to the fact that a certain group of tones is sung with a certain muscular adjustment of the vocal chords. At the points where the registers change, the vocal musculature readjusts itself automatically. This muscular change may disturb the beginner, who may then tighten the throat and try to force one muscular adjustment to do the work of two or more registers. This can be dangerous. But no trouble need be encountered if the student is particularly careful to:—

1 — RELAX THE THROAT.

2 — RELAX THE LOWER JAW.

3 — DEPEND ON BREATH CONTROL.

4 — TRY TO FEEL THE PLACE WHERE THE VOCAL VIBRATIONS OCCUR.

5 — OBSERVE THE SIMPLE RULES FOR THAT POINT OF CHANGE.

(Special exercises for singing smoothly through the registers are given later in the book.)

VOCAL CHORDS IN VIBRATION

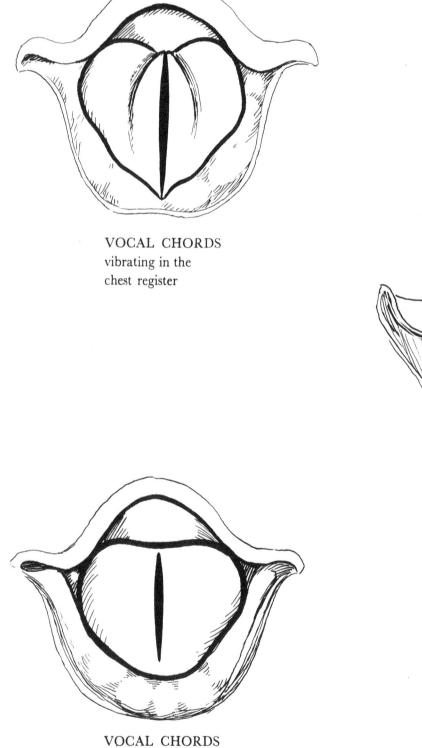

VOCAL CHORDS
vibrating in the
chest register

VOCAL CHORDS
vibrating in the
head register

VOCAL CHORDS
vibrating in the
medium register

THE RESONATING SYSTEM

All good musical instruments consist of a sound producing mechanism and a resonating system. In the singer the phonating system creates the actual sound itself. But this alone is quite weak and often unpleasant. Just ask an oboe or clarinet player to remove the mouthpiece of his instrument and blow a tone through it alone. You will be astonished and repelled by the harsh quality of tone it produces. But what a lovely sound that same tone has when the barrel of the instrument is attached! For the barrel contains the resonating system. The same thing applies to the voice.

In a resonating system we have two factors to consider: the material of which it is made and the air it contains. The singer is born with a resonating system and cannot change its construction materials. But parts of it can be somewhat manipulated to increase the amount of air they can contain.

Sound is conveyed by vibrations which can move quite freely through air and to a lesser degree through many hard materials. Soft materials are seldom good conductors of sound. To help visualize the sound vibrations in air, just recall the ripples that result when a pebble is dropped in water. Sound vibrations are ripples in the air, but they are much smaller and move much faster than water-ripples. As you have doubtless seen, water-ripples will continue to travel on into the distance until they die away or are stopped by some obstruction. Sound vibrations will act similarly. The problem of the singer, therefore, is to keep the resonators open so they will:—

1 — Beautify the tone.

2 — Allow the ripples in the air, the sound vibrations, to move freely outward into space. This is what we mean when we say that the voice is PROJECTED, or has CARRYING POWER.

For the sake of clarity we shall separate the singer's resonators into what we may call the primary and secondary types:—

1 — The primary type consists of the PHARYNX, and the TRACHEA and BRONCHIA. The pharynx is the soft throat passage itself and it extends roughly from the larynx up to the back of the nasal cavity. The trachea (windpipe) and bronchia (the air tubes of the lungs which converge into the trachea) are hard tubes made of cartilage.

2 — The secondary type of resonators is comprised of the mouth, nose and sinus chambers. These are encased in hard, bony material, with the exception of some parts of the mouth. The bones of the head and upper part of the chest are also secondary resonators.

Now, one opinion holds that the primary resonators are the only resonators, and that the secondary group has no such function, in fact, are of no value in singing. Well, it is true that the secondary resonators are farther away from the vocal chords, the actual producers of tone, and cannot be directly influenced by them. But long years of experience backs up the majority opinion that correct tone production will cause a distinct sensation of vibration in the front of the face, the mask, where the secondary resonators are mainly situated.

The great tenor Jean de Reszke was once asked if he had made any discoveries as to the key to fine singing. He answered, "I find that the great question of the singer's art becomes narrower and narrower all the time, until I can truly say that the great question of singing becomes a question of the nose." We hasten to add that de Reszke was NOT advocating nasal singing. We shall soon see what he meant.

A quick glance at the description of the resonators shows us that only the soft walls of the pharynx and the soft palate of the mouth are made of pliable material. That is, they can be moved at will. None of the other resonators can be manipulated. A nasal tone, therefore, results when the soft palate contracts and shuts off the nose cavity from the throat. Due to that obstruction the air in the nose does not vibrate. Consequently the tone cannot move outward but seems to stagnate in the nose. (A stuffed nose, due to a cold or a bad sinus condition will produce a similar effect.) The walls of the pharynx can. also contract and thereby greatly reduce the amount of vibrating air in the throat. This results in a throaty tone.

From this we can see that it is exceedingly important that the soft walls of the throat be OPEN and FREE from any muscular tightness. (Of course, a tight throat will also prevent the vocal chords from functioning properly.) And the soft palate must be in a similar open condition. To get the FEEL of the open throat and the raised soft palate:—

1 — Open the mouth in a relaxed manner and

2 — GENTLY INHALE THROUGH THE NOSE.

Thus, we see that what de Reszke meant was:—

1 — If the throat is open when we sing a tone,

2 — If the soft palate is gently raised, thus keeping the nasal chamber open,

3 — If we THINK the tone as directed towards the open nose,

4 — Then the vocal vibrations in the pharynx will be free to ripple through the air it contains on their way to the secondary resonators in the mask.

5 — Here they will be strengthened and colored by the additional air chambers, through which they will continue to ripple outwards towards the audience.

6 — The result will be a free, full-bodied, rich tone with great carrying power.

(It should be mentioned in passing that when singing a few tones in both the highest and lowest extremities of the voice, the soft palate will close the passage to the nasal chambers. But in these instances the vocal vibrations are conveyed to the "mask" by the bones of the head. This occurs AUTOMATICALLY and the pupil does not concern himself about it.)

THE ARTICULATING SYSTEM

The articulating system is composed of the various parts of the mouth and is concerned with the pronunciation of consonants and vowels, that is, "diction." The proper enunciation of those sounds requires the CONTROLLED RELAXATION of all the musculature of the face and mouth, especially the tongue and lips.

In addition, it is exceedingly important that the lower jaw SWING DOWN FREELY. Thus, when an open-mouthed vowel must be sung, the head should NOT be raised. Rather, the lower jaw must DROP DOWN. The hinges of the lower jaw lie at the sides of the head, just below the temples and in front of the ears. You can feel them move if you place your fingers on those points and move the lower jaw up and down.

During the days of Louis XIV, French drama, as well as French opera, had its golden age. It was at this time that the great playwrights and actors gave the French language its classical purity of pronunciation. And they coined a saying which we would do well to remember: "Do not exaggerate the vowels and you will speak beautifully. Honor the consonants and you will speak distinctly."

We can sing only on vowels. But the consonants not only help form words, they also help to place the vowel tone. Remember, consonants must be uttered with exactness, but quickly, so that the flowing tone may suffer as little interruption as possible. (But, when singing popular music it is effective to hold the consonants M, N and L a bit longer.)

At this point we will anticipate a matter of diction in order to discuss a vocal problem: — When the student has advanced to the point where the highest and lowest portions of the voice are being trained, the following may be noted:—

1 — Both extremes of the voice usually require a more OPEN position of the mouth. Therefore, if the mouth is not open and relaxed the result may be a forced and unpleasant sound.

2 — Consequently, if the student must sing a word with a "closed" vowel on either a high or a low tone, that vowel will have to be modified by "mixing" it with a more open vowel.

AH or O are the open vowels often used that way. For example: if the word POOL must be sung on a high tone, the lower jaw is dropped towards the position for AH or O, but the singer THINKS the vowel OO. The same applies for a low tone.

It is a remarkable fact that the original vowel will be AUTOMATICALLY pronounced if the singer THINKS it, that is, has a CLEAR MENTAL PICTURE of it.

The voice is the only musical instrument that combines words with music. The singer's diction therefore is exceedingly important and must be considered not only as a matter of good speech but as a musical problem as well. The student is strongly advised to study this subject intensively, for without fine diction he will never be able to rise to the top of the vocal profession.

In speech the mouth is opened sufficiently to allow the words to be easily and distinctly pronounced. Singing, however, requires a more open position of the mouth. But a soft tone does not require as open a position as a big tone. A little experimentation will quickly decide the size of the mouth opening for the best quality of tone.

The tongue, of course, moves in the pronunciation of the words. But, at no time should the tongue lie absolutely flat on the bottom of the mouth. If it does so, the back of the tongue will push against the larynx and obstruct the free emission of tone. Always keep the tongue flexible.

GENERAL REMARKS

1 — Soft singing and slow singing are the two most difficult things for the beginner. For they require the utmost control of the entire vocal mechanism. Therefore, unless and until otherwise instructed, ALL vocal exercises should be sung as follows: —

A — In a MEDIUM volume (not soft, not loud).

B — In a MODERATE tempo (not slow, not fast).

The beginner should never practise more than 15 minutes at a time. No voice lesson should exceed a half hour of actual singing.

2 — Sometimes it is difficult to recognize the precise voice-type of a beginner student. In most cases the voice is then gently but firmly developed up and down from the medium tones. But there are exceptions and in such instances the voice must be developed from its most beautiful tones, wherever those may appear. Generally, in a few weeks the natural inclination of the voice will display itself.

3 — Ultimately, the best results will be attained within the capabilities of the student. The singer should not be forced beyond his or her natural capacity in either range, volume or style.

4 — The word SUPPORT is an abbreviation of the expression BREATH SUPPORT and is often used as: "SUPPORT THE TONE". SUPPORT is of such great importance that it cannot be emphasized enough.

5 — PORTAMENTO means to SLUR (slide) from one tone to another. But the word "slur" is also the name of the curved line placed over or under a group of notes which must be played or sung smoothly — connectedly. This is called LEGATO and such a group of notes is known as a PHRASE. There is a world of difference between singing the notes of a phrase in a connected manner and sliding or slurring through those notes in portamento.

Legato singing is the basis of good, musicianly performance, but portamento is a device of style to be used with great discrimination. At first, only the teacher should decide where portamento should be used. Later, when the pupil becomes an artist, his good taste will be the guide in such matters. NEVER use the portamento twice in succession; that is absolutely forbidden. Only one slur at a time is permitted. In no composition will you see this: —

6 — When Caffarelli studied with the illustrious voice teacher Porpora, the latter kept him on a single page of vocalises for five years. At the end of that time Caffarelli set forth to become the greatest singer of the 18th century. From this we can draw two obvious conclusions: —

A — Even an unusually talented student must study intensively.

B — It is not necessary to study a multitude of exercises, but rather, a few well-chosen vocalises that are designed for specific purposes. In short, studies that will give the singer CONTROL, STRENGTH, DELICACY and FLEXIBILITY of voice.

The studies in this course have been selected with great care to achieve those objectives. (All purely musical matters are presented in another volume: GENERAL MUSICIANSHIP FOR THE SINGER.)

The student must understand that the teacher accompanies each exercise on the piano because: 1 — It helps the student achieve true pitch, that is, GOOD INTONATION. 2 — It helps the student realize that the tone or passage he or she sings is part of a larger harmonic structure. Thus, it improves his or her musical ear and MUSICIANSHIP. For these reasons most of the vocalises and their accompaniments are written out in their entirety in this book. (However, the teacher may have his or her own personal style of accompaniment for vocalises. In that case, the teacher should by all means use at the piano whatever accompaniment he or she may prefer.

Vocal studies are NOT taken up one week and discarded another week. They are studied consistently. But every experienced teacher knows that after a period of basic study certain exercises prove themselves most effective for certain students, while other exercises may be more effective for other students. Thus, from then on such exercises become the daily practise of those students and the means of "warming up" before auditions and performances.

REMEMBER: — Stand up in good posture while practising: shoulders down, chest out, stomach in. Relax the lower jaw — the mouth should be opened only by DROPPING the chin.

1

(Although the male low voices sound in the bass clef, the teacher may play the studies in the treble clef an octave higher.)

Middle C may be easier to sing if the student opens his mouth a bit more, i.e. drops the chin lower.

2

GOOD INTONATION means simply — absolute purity of pitch. Nothing sounds so unpleasant as a tone which is off-center — slightly sharp or flat.

THINK your tone as being directly in the center of the pitch.

(The vowel sounds in this study should have the Italian pronunciation — NAH-NEE.)

Keep the tempo moving: do not drag. (May be played an octave higher.)

Don't rush. Keep the tone flowing through the syllables.

Na Ni Na Ni Na Ni Na Ni Na   Na Ni Na Ni Na Ni Na Ni Na   Na Ni Na Ni Na Ni Na Ni Na
Si - a_____   Si - a_____   Si - a_____

Na Ni Na Ni Na Ni Na Ni Na   etc.
Si - a_____   etc.

(Baritones may stop here.)

4

Male singers, especially Baritones and Basses, sometimes have an inclination to want to sound "big" and virile and consequently may try to "push" the tone up from below. The result is a strain on the vocal chords, a forced, flat tone and the danger of ruining the voice. Take it easy (not necessarily a soft tone), relax, maintain GOOD BREATH SUPPORT and THINK the tone as coming down on the pitch FROM ABOVE.

When singing upwards THINK of the INTERVALS between the notes as being LARGER, and in downward passages as being SMALLER. Thus you will avoid singing flat. (It will not cause you to sing sharp.)

* Continue upward until C.

THE COVERED TONE

COVERING THE TONE implies a change, or rather a modification, of the vowel sound used when singing the upper tones. It is sometimes called a *mixed* vowel. In the Baritone and Bass voices this usually must take place from about D above Middle C (just above the bass clef) upwards. Covering the tone is a simple matter and involves the following:—

1 — Regardless of the vowel sound called for in the text of the song, the student must place his mouth in the position for the vowel AW.

2 — THINK the tone as aimed forward through the BRIDGE of the nose (that is, with a slight nasal quality).

3 — Keep the eyes looking straight ahead in a normal manner. (Some students tend to raise the eyebrows and look upward. This distorts the face which in turn tightens the throat muscles and prevents a free tone.)

4 — Do NOT force the tone "up from below", but rather think of the tone as easily coming down on the pitch FROM ABOVE.

5 — Maintain FULL BREATH SUPPORT. (Now, do not be fearful; go ahead and you will sing a fine, full-bodied "covered" tone.)

Should the student have some slight difficulty, he may start the tone with the vowel OO (as in FOOD). But as soon as the tone is produced he must DROP THE LOWER JAW to the position for AW. (Although OO helps to "place" the covered tone, it has the bad tendency of closing up the tone and preventing its free emission. This is true wherever it occurs in the voice. Therefore it is always modified, or mixed, with AW.)

It is a remarkable fact that even though you sing a mixed vowel on covered tones, if you THINK the original vowel of the text the audience will be fully conscious of it and be unaware of the mixture.

With the covered quality on the upper tones the latter will continue the color and resonance of the middle and lower registers. Without the covered tone the voice will sound "white", poor in quality, strained, and be in danger of cracking.

5

The syllable SOL should be pronounced as follows: — the letter S should be pronounced cleanly and quickly and move immediately to the vowel which should be pronounced AW. The final L should not be enunciated until the END of the last note.

6

The consonants should act to PLACE THE VOWELS FORWARD IN THE MOUTH.

7

(In all studies involving the highest tones of the voice the teacher must use care and fine judgment. The pupil should not be permitted to sing higher than he can go with ease, especially in the beginning. With time, the highest tones will develop. However, in some individuals such tones do not exist at all and, if force is used, the voice as a whole will suffer. This is especially true in the low voices.)

Flexibility and agility are as essential for the low voices as for the high voices. Almost all oratorios and many operas demand practically equal virtuosity from all the voice types. A Baritone or Bass who cannot sing a florid passage easily will find himself very limited in the vocal profession.

Remain in the position of the HIGHEST tone in each passage.

8

9

Sol Sol _____ Sol Sol____ (aw) _____

(cover) (cover)

Sol Sol____ (aw) _____ Sol Sawl _____ (ah) _____

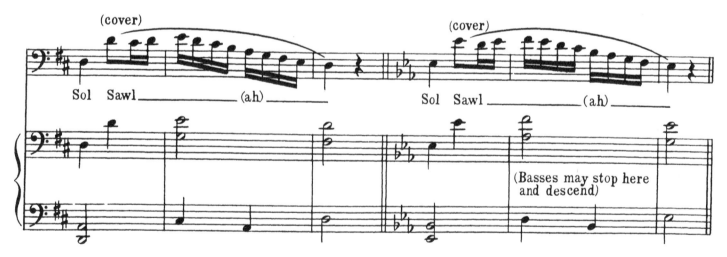

(cover) (cover)

Sol Sawl _____ (ah) _____ Sol Sawl _____ (ah) _____

(Basses may stop here and descend)

(cover) (cover)

Sol Sawl _____ (ah) _____ Sol Sawl _____ (ah) _____

(Baritones may go one or two ½-steps higher.)

Sol Sawl _____ (ah) ____ Sol Sawl _____ (ah) ____

Sol Sawl _____ (ah) ____ Sol Sawl ____ (ah) ____

Sol Sol ____ aw ____ (ah) ____ Sol Sol _____ (ah) ____

Sol Sol _____ (ah) ____ Sol Sol ____ (ah) ____

(Basses should continue
several tones lower.)

10

Sing each group of eight syllables with a perfectly steady tone, as if you were singing them all on one long note. Do NOT permit the tone to waver in pitch or quality. Keep the lip, tongue and lower jaw relaxed. Support with firm breath control. (Keep moving — do NOT drag the tempo.)

Do Re Mi Fa Sol La Si Do

SHORT BREATHS

Sing the following exercise like this:—

1 — Take a SHORT breath and sing the five tones in ONE BREATH.

2 — HOLD the last note as long as you can.

Ma   Ma   Ma   Ma   Ma

Try to feel how much breath you took for the above passage. Now take the SAME amount of breath and sing the seven notes just as you sang the five.

Ma   Ma   Ma   Ma   Ma   Ma   Ma

Take the SAME amount of breath and, in the SAME way, sing the nine notes.

Ma   Ma   Ma   Ma   Ma   Ma   Ma   Ma   Ma

Take the SAME amount of breath and, in the SAME way, sing the eleven notes.

Ma   Ma   Ma   Ma   Ma   Ma   Ma   Ma   Ma   Ma   Ma

If you have been breathing correctly you should have no difficulty with these studies. If you have been able to sing the eleven notes with the same quantity of breath you took for the five notes, then obviously you took too much breath for those five.

The object of the above exercise is to make you realize that: it is not necessary to take a "lot of breath", but rather to take what you NEED and use it properly. Remember — for short phrases take short breaths; for long phrases take long breaths.

(These exercises may also be used as studies in sustained tones.)

11

Be very careful of the intonation in this chromatic study. (Don't drag the tempo.)

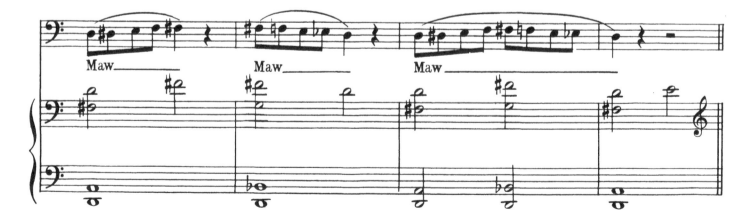

Maw_____ Maw_____ Maw_____

Maw_____ Maw_____ Maw_____

Maw_____ Maw_____ Maw_____

Maw_____ Maw_____ Maw_____

12

All voices must be able to sing easily throughout their entire ranges. But, as the Basses establish the harmonic foundation, their low tones are somewhat more important than the low tones of the other voices. Now, as the low tones have the slowest rate of vibration, obviously a greater degree of RELAXATION of the entire vocal mechanism is necessary. This is true of all voices. However, since Basses are required to produce their low tones more often than the other voices, they must be able to relax into those low tones more quickly than the other voices. For these reasons Basses should NOT END ON HIGH TONES IN THEIR STUDIES. Instead, they should immediately follow the final high tones with a few passages from MEDIUM TO LOW TONES. (Baritones may do the same, but it is not as essential for them.)

Interestingly enough, in the case of the lowest tones, as with the highest tones, the vowels of the text should be MIXED with AW. When singing the LOWEST tones: 1 — Point the lips forward (especially the lower lip). 2 — RELAX the abdominal muscles a bit. 3 — Mix the vowels with AW.

14

Sawl _____
Faw _____

Sawl _____
Faw _____

(Basses start here)

Sawl _____
Faw _____

Sawl _____
Faw _____

Sol _____
Fa _____

Sol _____
Fa _____

(cover)   (cover)

Sol _____ (aw) _____ (ah) _____   Sol _____ (aw) _____ (ah) _____
Fa _____ (aw) _____ (ah) _____   Fa _____ (aw) _____ (ah) _____

(Baritones start here)

(cover)   (cover)

Sol _____ (aw) _____ (ah) _____   Sol _____ (aw) _____ (ah) _____
Fa _____ (aw) _____ (ah) _____   Fa _____ (aw) _____ (ah) _____

(Basses end here)

(cover)   (cover)

Sol _____ (aw) _____ (ah) _____   Sol _____ (aw) _____ (ah) _____
Fa _____ (aw) _____ (ah) _____   Fa _____ (aw) _____ (ah) _____

(cover)   (cover)

Sol _____ (aw) _____ (ah) _____   Sol _____ (aw) _____ (ah) _____
Fa _____ (aw) _____ (ah) _____   Fa _____ (aw) _____ (ah) _____

15

Maintain a full, free-flowing tone with a smooth, easy production.

Remember: On the lowest tones — POINT THE LIPS FORWARD (especially the lower lip), RELAX THE ABDOMINAL MUSCLES A BIT, MODIFY THE VOWELS WITH AW.

Keep the voice in the position of the HIGHEST tone in each passage. Even for the lowest notes you must feel that your tone is coming down on the pitch from ABOVE.

(Don't drag the tempo — keep moving. Play the R.H. an octave higher than written.)

L.H. an octave lower

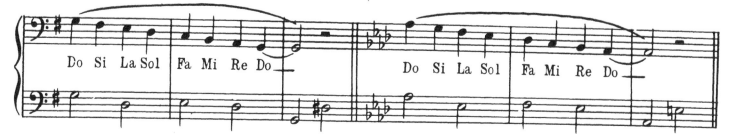

Do Si La Sol Fa Mi Re Do   Do Si La Sol Fa Mi Re Do

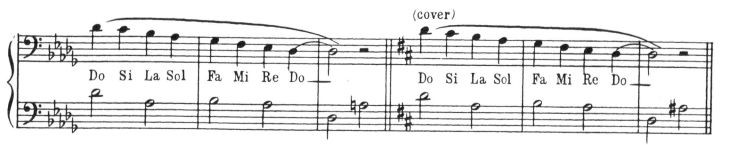

Do Si La Sol Fa Mi Re Do   Do Si La Sol Fa Mi Re Do

Do Si La Sol Fa Mi Re Do   Do Si La Sol Fa Mi Re Do

(cover)

Do Si La Sol Fa Mi Re Do   Do Si La Sol Fa Mi Re Do

(cover)   (cover)

Do Si La Sol Fa Mi Re Do   Do Si La Sol Fa Mi Re Do
(Basses end here and D. C. al Fine)   (Bar. continue)

(cover)   (cover)

Do Si La Sol Fa Mi Re Do   Do Si La Sol Fa Mi Re Do

Keep this study moving fairly fast. It should be sung lightly but with a firm tone supported with good breath control. The accents should be merely slightly emphasized — not exaggerated.

Sol Fa_____ Sol Fa_____ Sol Fa_____
(Basses return here - to Fine) (Baritones continue next page)

L.H. an octave lower

Sol Fa _____ (aw) Sol Fa_____ (aw) Sol Fa ___ (aw)

Sol Fa_____ (aw)__ Sol Faw_____ Sol Faw_____ FINE for Basses

Sol Faw_____ Sol Faw_____ Sol Fa_____ (aw)__

Sol Fa_____ (aw) Sol Fa _____ (aw) Sol Fa_____

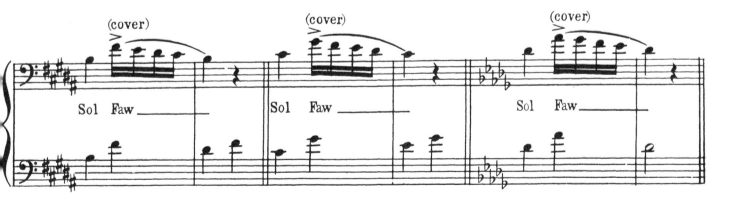

42

Keep the tones easy and as resonant as possible. Remember — come down on the tone from ABOVE.

(Basses begin here). Play R.H. an octave higher.

(Baritones may start here)

Basses end here

(Basses sing a few low tones now)

MESSA DI VOCE means the ability to start a tone SOFT, swell it to LOUD and diminish it back to SOFT. (Not to be confused with Mezza Voce which merely means Half-Voice, or SOFT.) The following study consists of a number of steps aiming towards the achievement of a fine Messa Di Voce.

1 — Start medium soft and gradually swell the tone to medium loud.

2 — Start medium loud and diminish to medium soft.

3 — Start medium soft, swell to medium loud, diminish to medium soft.

4 — Start very soft and swell to a full, big tone.

5 — Start with a full, big tone and diminish to a soft, velvety tone.

6 — Start very soft, swell to very loud, diminish to very soft.

Throughout these studies keep a RELAXED LOWER JAW and THROAT and above all — maintain FULL BREATH SUPPORT. (If your throat tightens, the tone will crack. Should this happen, stop immediately, take a fresh breath and do the passage again.)

(The teacher will use his or her own judgment about extending these studies lower and higher.)

THE HEAD VOICE

As we have previously noted (page 13) the head register in male singers is not a "regular" part of the male voice as it is in the female voice, because: 1 — the pure head tones in the male voice have a different quality from those in the lower registers; 2 — the male head tones are weak and have little carrying power. For these reasons some teachers and singers ignore the male head voice. Although it is true that the male singer does not necessarily require a head voice, nevertheless this register is of some value. We shall therefore state here its advantages and drawbacks and leave the matter to the judgment of the teacher.

Since the pure male head tone cannot be produced with force it is of benefit when used as a relaxing study in the case of those students who tend to clutch, or constrict, the throat muscles. It can rise very high, higher than the highest full-voice tones and it can be brought down to the middle of the medium register. Most authorities are generally agreed that this type of tone is produced by the thin edges only of the vocal chords. Nowadays this kind of tone is also referred to as Falsetto. But we repeat, it is normally weak. Therefore, when it is used in a song it is for the purpose of producing a soft, velvety tone quality on a pianissimo note. It is quite effective when used that way. It is also used that way by vocal ensembles. The drawback in the male head voice lies in its misuse, which comes about as follows: It is possible, through practise, to so strengthen the upper head tones as to give them what might be called a "false" tenor brilliance. Singers who do this are then under the mistaken impression that they have extended their range of high tones. But this is NOT true because such tones are risky and difficult to control and also, such tones can NEVER be blended downward into the medium register. An unpleasant BREAK will always occur in such instances.

When the head voice is used in a song it should only be employed WITHIN THE LIMITS OF THE UPPER MEDIUM REGISTER. In summary, it may be stated that:—

1 — Practise of head tones is of benefit because they can be produced only with a completely RELAXED THROAT and GOOD BREATH CONTROL. (Any tension whatsoever will prevent their production.)

2 — The head voice has its place in the male singer when an especially soft, sweet tone is called for in the upper medium register. But the singer must not think he should use it on all soft tones or his singing will lose its characteristic masculine quality. (Outside of its use as an occasional stylistic touch, the head tones have no other value in a song.)

Keep the lower jaw, lips and tongue completely relaxed. Keep a pleasant expression. Maintain full breath support. Sing the tone very softly and place it further back in the head than the regular tone, thus eliminating the frontal resonance. A more floating sound will then be produced. (Should there be any difficulty at first, use a little puff of air on the letter H instead of L to get the tone started.)

The teacher may extend these studies a few tones higher if he wishes.

STYLE

What is style? "The application of the laws of artistic taste to the interpretation of music". Acquire the habit of singing beautifully even though you sing only a scale. Music is music, whether it be on the page of an exercise book or in an opera score. Until voice placing and technique are secure, attempts to acquire style are premature. But, without style, a well placed voice and good technique are not enough. And until the singer's education is rounded out into a repertoire adapted to his talent, voice and specific capabilities, he is not ready for the public.

Of all the elements of style in singing, the most effective is color. The composer creates tone color by change of key and chord, by clever use of the various "sound effects" existing in the instrument he is writing for, and by change of dynamics. The singer must follow the written music. But the voice, the singer's instrument, is capable of a greater range of "sound effects" than any other instrument. The singer must color the voice to match the meaning of all important words. Sorrow, rage, despair, joy, tenderness, every noun and every adjective in every language, can stir the sensitive singer to the use of the proper tone color for that particular portrayal. Because of this remarkable capacity of the voice for tone color, we often find an orchestra conductor asking his instrumentalists to "sing" a passage, that is, to try to imitate the voice on their instruments.

To be a great singer, there must be: —

1 — Perfect breath control and technique.

2 — Perfect diction.

3 — Absolute accuracy of intonation.

4 — Appropriate vocal coloring of each sentiment expressed.

5 — A beautiful cantilena (smooth, flowing melody line).

6 — A perfect messa di voce.

7 — Discreet use of portamento.

8 — Perfect execution of difficult ornamentation (trills, turns, runs, etc.).

9 — An education which enables you to understand the meaning of the text which inspired the composition.

10 — The talent and ability to impart to the audience what you feel and think.

SPECIAL PROBLEMS

No teacher can pursue a pedagogic career without encountering special problems on the way. All voices are not equally fortunate in having escaped mishaps. For one thing, sometimes unfortunate handling of the voice has resulted in incorrect placing of high tones. Sometimes the high tones are missing altogether. (However, it is wise to remember that some singers have by nature "short voices" and never can acquire an extended high range.) Then there are cases where the middle register has been impaired and shows a strained quality. Further, a singer may have developed a tremolo or may have trouble with intonation. The following practical suggestions should prove beneficial in such cases.

Problems of High and Medium Tones

Humming is of inestimable value in instances where there is difficulty in achieving high tones and also where the medium voice is strained and poor in quality. Sing the hum as HM and keep the lips LOOSELY closed. The following studies should be sung lightly and easily but firmly. 1 — For the sake of the high tones start the studies as written and move upwards by half-steps, gradually extending the range over a period of a number of lessons. 2 — For work on the medium tones, start as written and move downward a few half-steps and then upward, just keeping to the middle register.

Tremolo

A voice may develop tremolo from one of several reasons: —

1 — Too much singing, resulting in fatigue of the vocal chords.

2 — Singing songs in the wrong range (too high or too low).

3 — Bad breath support.

Since it is hard to decide immediately what has caused the tremolo, the wise thing for the teacher to do is to insist upon complete rest of the vocal chords for a number of days. Then begin study with the humming exercises given above. After this use the study for "short" breaths on page 29.

Faulty Intonation

A faulty sense of pitch may be due to a "bad ear", in which case it is often practically a hopeless condition. However, it may be due to psychological reasons which show themselves in a subconscious fear on the part of the student to express himself freely and a consequent holding back so the pitch is insecure. If, after attempting to develop a sense of pitch in the pupil by technical and other means, the teacher finds that the poor intonation continues, it would be wiser to advise the student to give up singing.

But sometimes bad intonation is due to faulty voice placing or to clumsy diction. In such cases VERY CAREFULLY PRONOUNCED SYLLABLES will help to place a tone in the correct spot so that the intonation is perfect. And sometimes, where the diction is not good, CAREFUL ATTENTION TO THE CORRECT PLACING OF THE TONE will improve the diction and help the singer sing in tune. It is practically an interchangeable process.

Interpretation

Young singers should be taught to understand the meaning of the text before they learn the music of a song. Sometimes it is necessary, when the words do not inspire them sufficiently, to stir them with the beauty of the music. On the other hand, if a song means to them only the music and they chant monotonously (even though the sounds are beautiful), they must be taught to use their minds as well as their vocal talent.

Students should be taught to be sparing in the use of cadenzas, ornaments and other embellishments which the composer himself did not include in the composition. Anything which is overdecorated is in bad taste.

PART III — DICTION

MEND YOUR VOICE A LITTLE, LEST YOU MAR YOUR FORTUNE.

William Shakespeare

Singing is so intimately bound up with words that we feel it to be of great importance that the student make the study of diction an integral part of his vocal training. For this reason we present here the fundamentals of correct pronunciation for the five languages most commonly used in singing: English, Italian, French, German and Spanish.

ENGLISH

The following descriptions are based on what authorities call STANDARD English. This is the diction used by most actors, public speakers and especially the announcers of the big radio and television networks. Listen to those speakers carefully and check your pronunciation against theirs. (Some announcers on small stations use the local accents or inflections to which their ear has become accustomed. It is not safe to use them as speech models.) Remember, you want to be understood by everyone, not just your home town neighbors. (There is nothing wrong with speaking in your local manner at home and among friends — but use STANDARD pronunciation in all singing except in folk or dialect songs.)

Vowels

Pure vowels preserve the position of the vocal organs in the production of tone. When this is disturbed by bad vowel pronunciation, the movements of the lips and tongue become distorted in forming the consonants and are serious obstacles to good singing.

The English language has a great many vowel sounds, but unfortunately we cannot always recognize them from the spelling of the words in which they appear. In elementary school we are told that the vowels are: A, E, I, O, U and sometimes Y. But each of these has several sounds and some are combined with others, as we shall see. Although the basic vowels are easily recognized, many others require a good ear for their detection. Learn to LISTEN to the vowel sounds you pronounce and do not be careless in your pronunciation.

Vowels are shaped either by the tongue or by the lips. In both cases they are aided by the lower jaw. But above all, remember that vowels are OPEN sounds. Therefore the mouth parts used in consonants are not used here and MUST NOT interfere with the pure pronunciation of the vowels. Their proper enunciation requires the utmost flexibility of the relaxed tongue, lips and lower jaw.

Tongue Vowels

There are five main tongue positions and each produces a distinct vowel. In the tongue vowels the lips are completely relaxed and not shaped. The lower jaw helps a bit by moving up or down as the tongue positions get higher or lower. The five tongue vowels, moving from low to high tongue and jaw positions are:—

A (AH) as in MAMA (FATHER)

A   as in FAT

E   as in MET

I   as in SIT

E (EE) as in ME (MEET)

Lip Vowels

In the lip vowels the tongue moves hardly at all. The lips actually do not move either, but are RELAXED and slightly PROTRUDED. (It is because of this slight protrusion that certain vowels are formed and hence the name.) We repeat, the lips do not move; but the vowels are produced by the lower jaw as it moves up or down. The five lip vowels, moving from low to high jaw position are:—

A (AW) as in FALL
U as in BUT
U (UR) as in YEARN
U as in PULL
OO as in FOOL

Vowel Combinations

A number of vowel sounds are in reality combinations of two vowels. They are called:—

Diphthongs

AH + EE as in LIGHT
AY + EE as in SAY
AW + I as in SOIL
AH + OO as in ROUND
AW + OO as in SO
A + U(R) as in FAIR
EE + U(R) as in FEAR
OO + U(R) as in SURE

Combinations of three vowels are called:—

Triphthongs

AH + OO + U(R) as in HOUR
AH + EE + U(R) as in MIRE

When singing diphthongs and triphthongs be sure to clearly enunciate each vowel in the combination. However, they do NOT all receive equal time. Thus, in both a diphthong and a triphthong the FIRST vowel is always the most important. It gets most of the time-value of the note or notes on which it occurs. However, just before you must go on to the next word, you add the remaining one or two vowels. But, quickly as you add the latter, you must make them distinct. If they are omitted the word is distorted and even the meaning changed. For example:

NIGHT, without the quick EE after the long AH, becomes NOT.

OUR, without the quick OO + U(R) after the long AH, becomes ARE.

Consonants

Generally, the pronunciation of consonants, with a few exceptions, presents no difficulties. Also, unlike vowels which are often pronounced differently in different localities, consonants only rarely lend themselves to local distortions. Therefore we shall present here mainly those consonants having exceptional features that require special attention:—

In English, double consonants make NO difference in pronunciation; we consider only one of them. Thus, in the word BERRY only one R is pronounced. And the same applies to: LITTLE = LITLE, FOLLOW = FOLOW, etc.

We must place a neutral sounding vowel between adjoining consonants such as PL in PEOPLE, TL in LITTLE, etc. Without a neutral vowel those consonants will have unpleasant sounds. The neutral vowel is usually UH (the U as in BUT), but it should not be exaggerated.

Final consonants should have NO following vowel sounds. However, there are three exceptions: B, D and Hard G (as in GO). These must be followed by a VERY SHORT neutral vowel sound or they will not be heard: MOB = MOB(uh), LED = LED(uh), LEG = LEG(uh). Do NOT prolong this neutral vowel.

Generally, consonants occurring in the middle of words, that is, preceded and followed by vowels, are treated as follows:— the middle consonant does NOT close the preceding syllable — it BEGINS the new syllable. For example: WRITING = WRI-TING, FELLOW = FE-LOW, etc. (The dictionary requires those words to be written thus when broken: writ-ing, fel-low, etc. But in pronunciation, especially in singing, we ignore this and follow the rule given here.)

The humming consonants M and N are very beautiful and, when properly used, enrich the vocal sound. They are therefore prolonged in singing wherever possible. Authorities are generally agreed that they should be held for HALF the time-value of the note. But, if the note has a length of three beats, then the humming consonant is placed on the third count.

An IMPLOSION occurs in ordinary clear speech when a word, ending in an explosive consonant, is followed by a word beginning with a sung consonant, both consonants being pronounced by the same mouth parts. For example: THAT DOOR. In speech, the final T would not be exploded, but instead a sudden stop occurs and a new start is made on the next word. The sudden silence brought on by the stop is the implosion. This is NOT good practise in singing. Instead, the tone must be carried through the sung consonant beginning the second word: in the above example, the D.

Sung and Unsung Consonants

UNSUNG consonants are of three types: — explosive, sibilant and aspirate. They have NO tone quality. (Such a consonant is also called a SURD.)

1 — The explosive consonants are CH (as in CHIN), K, P and T. Their enunciation causes a tiny explosion of air, hence their name.

2 — The sibilant consonants are F, H, S, SH, WH (as in WHAT) and TH (as in TEETH). The air that creates them is clearly heard.

The SUNG consonants are: B, D, G (as in GO), G (as in GENEROUS), J, L, M, N, NG (as in SINGING), R, S (as in LEISURE), TH (as in THAT), W (as in WON) and Y (as in YOUNG). These have a definite tone quality and each has the SAME PITCH as the VOWEL which it accompanies. (Such a consonant is also called a SONANT.)

The Letter R

The letter R has some unusual problems which require special consideration.

Hard R

The Hard R, in general speech, is heard mainly in England. Used to extremes it makes SORRY sound like SODDY; but it should not be that hard:—

1 — The tip of the tongue quickly and lightly FLICKS the rim of the gum just behind the upper front teeth.

2 — As the tongue-tip flips down in its flicking action, sing the tone of the vowel sounding with the R.

Do NOT roll or trill the tongue in English. (However, most other languages do trill the R.)

Soft R

The Soft R, in general speech, is used mainly in the United States and Canada.

The tip of the tongue merely POINTS towards the rim of the upper front gum; it does NOT touch anything.

Broadly speaking, the Hard R should be used only in opera because it has greater carrying power. This is necessary in opera houses which are usually large and where microphones are not used to amplify the singer's voices. In radio and television, since "mikes" are used, the Soft R is preferable.

In sacred music both types are employed: generally the Soft R is used; but in the case of those words which convey religious sentiment, such as SACRED, the Hard R is preferred as it has more dignity.

The Soft R should be used in all other types of singing: concert, musical comedy, popular and operetta (except in Gilbert and Sullivan, where the Hard R is traditional).

General Rules for R

1 — OMIT the R sound when it occurs before a consonant, whether the consonant is part of the same word or the beginning of a new word. For example:—

FOR ME = FAW ME

FORTY = FAWTY

Do NOT shorten, or clip, the word or syllable because the R is omitted. Rather, LENGTHEN the vowel preceding it.

2 — OMIT the final R. For example: — MOTHER = MOTH-UH. (This is not true for most foreign languages.)

3 — Always pronounce the R when it precedes a vowel. For example:

FURROW = FU-ROW. The same treatment is used when a word with a final R is followed by a word beginning with a vowel. For example:—

ARE IN = AH-RIN. Such word combinations are treated as single words having a middle R before a vowel.

The only exception to this rule occurs in words ending in a silent vowel. For example: — ARE = AH.

FOREIGN LANGUAGE DICTION

In the foreign languages presented in the following pages most of the speech sounds are similar to those in English. But of course they are put together in combinations that make different kinds of word-sounds. However, there are a few very important differences. The differences among consonants will be taken up in their proper places. But the differences among vowels must be mentioned here or we will not have a clear conception of how they sound and our approach to the languages will be incorrect.

The four main vowel differences are: The Nasal vowels used in French, the Tongue-Lip vowels used in French and German, the Short E and the Short O. The first two groups will be discussed in our outlines of French and German. But the others must be described now as they occur in all the languages presented here.

The Short E is somewhat like the E used in the English word YET. However, it does have a slight Ay (as in WAY) sound. But the latter must be so faint as to be barely heard. It merely gives the Short E a tiny, turned-up quality. Perhaps our EH would be closer to the true foreign sound.

Although the Long O (as in HOPE) is occasionally used in most languages, the Short O is the commonest and most important. It may be compared to the Short AW (as in SHORT). Use the Short O unless otherwise indicated. The student is strongly advised to obtain a good dictionary of the foreign language he is studying.

Italian

Italian		*English*

VOWELS

A	pronounced		AH (as in FATHER)
E	pronounced	short	EH (as in YET)
I	pronounced		EE (as in MEET)
O	pronounced	short	AW (as in SHORT)
U	pronounced		OO (as in POOL)
AI	pronounced	long	I (as in MINE)
IU	pronounced		U (as in PURE)

CONSONANTS

C followed by E or I		CH (as in CHESS)
CH		K (as in KISS)
(example: CHIARO = KEE-AH-RAW)		
G (followed by E or I)		J (as in JELLY)
(example: GELOSO = JEL-O-ZO)		
G (followed by other vowels)	hard	G (as in GO)
GH	hard	G (as in GO)
H		always silent
J		Y (as in YELLOW)
(example: REJETTA = RAY-YET-TAH)		
R		always trilled
S (between two vowels)		Z (as in LAZY)
(otherwise S is the same as in English)		
There is no W in Italian. Its place is taken by UO.		
Z		DZ
(example: ZIO = DZEE-O)		
ZZ		TS (as in NUTS)
(example: VEZZO = VETSO)		

COMBINED CONSONANTS

SCI	SHEE
SCE	SHEH
SCHI	SKEE
SCHE	SKEH

G before L or N followed by a vowel is ignored
and Y is inserted after the L or N. For example:
GLI = LYEE, FIGLI = FEEL-YEE
OGNI = AWN-YEE, DEGNO = DEHN-YO

DOUBLE CONSONANTS

Double consonants are pronounced HARDER and the preceding vowel is shortened slightly so as to anticipate the first of the two consonants.
(examples: beLla, doNna, tuTti)

French

French has more vowel sounds than the other languages here discussed. French, like English, has so many exceptions to general rules of pronunciation that the student would do well to obtain a good English-French dictionary (CASSELL'S or OXFORD). In addition, it is wise to remember that in French no syllable is stressed or accented unless a specific indication is given.

	French	*English*

VOWELS

The vowel A is generally pronounced AH (as in FATHER). But it is often pronounced short, as in AN (AT, CAT). (Consult the dictionary.)

I	EE (as in MEET)
O	short AW (as in SHORT)
Y	EE (as in MEET)

The vowel E has several pronunciations according to the type of sign over it and according to where it appears in a word:—

É (acute accent)	short EY (as in THEY)
ER, ET, EZ (ending a word)	short EY (as in THEY)
È (grave accent)	E (like E in THERE)
Ê (caret)	short E (as in MET)

COMBINED VOWELS

AI	AI (as in FAIR)
AU (also EAU)	long O (as in ROSE)
EI	short A (as in PLAN)
OU	long OO (as in FOOD)
OI	WAH (OO + AH)

(example: NOIR = NWAHR)

FINAL M
FINAL N

M and N at the beginning of a word or between two vowels is pronounced as in English. But M or N before a consonant or at the end of a word is not pronounced at all but becomes NASAL. That is, the tone of the voice is directed through the NOSE instead of through the mouth as in all other speech sounds. We shall use the reverse arrow for the nasal sound — (<). For example:—

	TROMPER	TRAW<-PAY
	FONCER	FAW<-SAY
These are all	AN	AH<
pronounced	EM	same as above
the same.	EN	same as above
	UN	A (A as in AN)
	ON	AW<

TONGUE-LIP VOWELS

The French vowel U has no counterpart in English. It is pronounced as follows:—

1 — Make the tongue flat to pronounce the long vowel EE.

2 — Point the lips as if you were going to whistle.

You must COMBINE THE FLAT TONGUE WITH THE POINTED LIPS.
To denote that sound we shall use this sign — E>

The combined vowels EU (also OEU) combines the tongue position for AY with the pointed lips. For that sound we shall use this sign — AY>

SINGLE L
DOUBLE LL   A Single L or Double LL preceded by I is omitted and only the preceding vowel or vowel combination is pronounced.

ILLE . . . . EE
    (example: FILLE = FEE)

EIL . . . . AY
    (example: SOLEIL = SAW-LAY)

EILLE . . . . AY
    (example: VEILLE = VAY)

AIL . . . . AH-EE
    (example: TRAVAIL = TRAH-VAH-EE)

AILLE . . . . AH-EE
    (example: MURAILLE = ME>-RAH-EE)

EUIL (also OEIL) . . . . AY>
    (example: FAUTEUIL = FO-TAY>)

UEILLE . . . . AY>
    (example: CUEILLE = KAY>)

When Double LL is preceded by I and followed by another syllable beginning with a vowel then the Double LL becomes Y.

BRILLIANT = BREE-YAH<
VEILLER   = VAY-YAY
MOUILLER = MOO-YAY

However, there are a few exceptions where the L sound is distinctly pronounced. There seems to be no rule for this, so the student should consult the English-French dictionary. For example:

TRANQUILLE = TRAH<-KEEL
VILLAGE   = VEE-LAHZH
VILLE   = VEEL

G before N followed by a vowel is ignored and Y is inserted after the N. (This is the same as in Italian.)
    (example: SEIGNEUR SAYN-YAI>R)

CONSONANTS

C (before E or I) . . . . S (as in SISTER)
C (before other vowels) . . . . K
Ç (wherever used) . . . . S (as in SISTER)
    (example: REÇU = REH-SE>)
G (before E, I or Y) . . . . ZH (like S in PLEASURE)
    (example: GEORGE = ZHORZH)
J . . . . ZH (like S in PLEASURE)
G (before other vowels) . . . . hard G (as in GO)

H is usually silent. However, about 25% of the time it is aspirated as in English. There seems to be no rule for it and it should be looked up in the dictionary for correct pronunciation of the word in which it appears. For example:

(LA) HONTE = HAUNT
HABIT = AH-BEE

However, H is always silent when preceded by L apostrophe.

L'HEURE = LEU>R

QU . . . . K (never KW)
    (examples: QUE = KU>, QUI = KEE)
    QUERELLE = KER-ELL

R is guttural (throaty) in spoken French, but always trilled when sung.

S (between two vowels) . . . . Z (as in CAUSE)
S (elsewhere) . . . . hard S (as in SISTER)
TH . . . . T
    (example: THÉÂTRE = TAY-ATR-RUH)

French (*Continued*)

In a final syllable TI is pronounced like S. For example:—

MARTIAL = MAHR-SEE-AHL
PARTIEL = PAHR-SEE-EL
ACTION = AHK-SEE-AW<

W . . . . V (as in VERY)
  (example: WAGON = VAH-GAW<)
X (preceded by I) . . . . SS (as in KISS)
  (examples: SIX = SEESS, DIX = DEESS)
In all other cases X is pronounced KS or GZ as in English.
  (examples: EXTRÈME = EKS-TREM
             EXONERER = EG-ZUN-ER-AY

DOUBLE CONSONANTS

When double GG is followed by E or I the first G is hard, the second, soft. For example:—

SUGGERER = SU>G-ZHAY-RAY

Double GG followed by any other letter is always HARD.

AGGRAVÉ = AG-RAH-VAY
CH (followed by L or R) . . . . K
  (examples: CHLORAL = KLAW-RAHL, CHROME = KRAWM)
CH (otherwise) . . . . always SH (as in English)
  (example: CHOSE = SHOHZ)

Double MM and double NN are pronounced as in English. In the combination MN, the M is ignored and only the N is pronounced.

AUTOMNE = O-TUN

FINAL CONSONANTS

Final consonants are usually silent, that is, not pronounced.

CHAUD = SHO
CLEF = KLAY

Final ANT and ENT are both pronounced AH< (nasal).

POURTANT = POOR-TAH<
COMMENT = KAW-MAH<

There is the grammatical ending ENT which is ignored. It is the third person plural. This is a verb ending.

AIMENT = AYM

When sung on two unslurred notes = AYM-UH
However, final consonants are pronounced if the following word starts with a vowel. Then the two words are connected and pronounced as one word. This is called the Liaison (LEE-AY-ZAW<).

ELLES AIMENT = EL-ZEM
TOUT A FAIT = TOO-TAH-FAY

Final E causes the preceding consonant to be clearly pronounced. But it also causes the vowel sound before that consonant to be shortened. Compare each pair of words in the following:—

TRAIN = TRA<   PLEIN = PLA<
TRAINE = TRENN   PLEINE = PLENN

But sometimes the penultimate vowel is long, as in: UNE = EE>N, QUINZE = KA<Z

German

(There are several good, inexpensive paper bound German dictionaries.)

	German	English
VOWELS	A	AH (as in FATHER)
	E (before ONE consonant)	short EY (as in THEY)
	E (before TWO consonants)	short E (as in MET)
	E (followed by H)	long AY (as in WAY)
	I (between consonants)	short I (as in SIT)
	I (followed by H)	long EE (as in MEET)
	O (before ONE consonant)	short O (as in LOVE)
	O (before TWO consonants)	UH (as in UP)
	O (followed by H)	long O (as in ROSE)
	U (before ONE consonant)	long OO (as in FOOD)
	U (before TWO consonants)	short OO (as in FOOT)

Y is rarely used in German. Before a consonant it is long EE. Before a vowel it is pronounced as in English.

	German	English
DOUBLE VOWELS	IE	EE (as in MEET)
	EI	long I (as in MINE)
	EU	short OY (as in BOY)
	AU	OW (as in COW)

THE UMLAUT

The umlaut is a double dot placed horizontally over certain words. In the letters O and U it creates the Tongue-Lip vowels in German. Here again, as with the French U and Tongue-Lip vowels, we use our sign ⊃, meaning: keep the lips pointed as for whistling, while the tongue is in the position for the vowel.

Ä .... EH
    (example: GÄRTNER = GEHRTNER)

ÄU .... OY ⊃
    (example: BÄUERIN = BOY⊃-ERIN)

Ö (before ONE consonant) .... AY ⊃
    (example: BÖSER = BAY⊃-ZER)

Ö (before TWO consonants) ...... short EH ⊃
    (examples: HÖLLE = HEH⊃-LE, OFFNEN = EH⊃F-NEN)

Ü .... E ⊃
    (example: FÜSSE = FE⊃-SUH)

CONSONANTS

C (before A, O or U) .... K

C (before E or I) .... TS (as in NUTS)
    (example: CITRONE = TSIT-RO-NE⊃)

G is always hard .... G (as in GO)
    (example: GEORG = GAY-ORG)

J .... Y
    (example: JA = YAH)

S (at the beginning of a word) .... Z
    (example: SONNE = ZUN-NE⊃)

S (at the end of a syllable or before a consonant) . S (as in WEST)

Double SS is pronounced more sharply.

SZ .... SS

S (before P or T at the beginning of a word) ... SH (as in SHELL)
    (examples: STUHL = SHTOOL, SPIEGEL = SHPEE-GEL)

S (before P or T in the middle or end of a word) . S (as in English)
    (example: FINSTER = FINS-TER)

German (*Continued*)

V . . . . hard F (as in OFF)
(example: VOR = FOR)

W . . . . V (as in VERY)
(example: WISSEN = VISS-EN)

Z . . . . TS (as in NUTS)
(example: ZITTER = TSIT-TER)

COMBINED CONSONANTS

SCH . . . . SH (as in SHELL)

TSCH . . . . CH (as in CHESS)

QU . . . . KV
(example: QUAL = KVAHL)

PF is distinctly and separately pronounced.
(example: APFEL = AHP-FEL)

CH (followed by S) . . . . X (as in English)
(example: OCHSEN = OX-SEN)

CH rarely begins a word. When it does, it may be pronounced either as K or as SH. There is no rule for this; it must be looked up in a German-English dictionary.

examples: CHERUB = KAY-ROOB
CHAMPAGNER = SHAHM-PAHN-YER

CH also has two other pronunciations which have no counterpart in English:—

A — CH after E, I and UR is soft and is pronounced as follows:—

1 — Make the tongue flat.
2 — Touch the sides of the tongue to the upper side teeth.
3 — The front of the tongue does NOT touch anything.
4 — Aim a stream of air against the HARD PALATE just BEHIND the front upper teeth.
5 — The escaping air should be heard. (Do NOT aim the breath directly at the front teeth or you will get the English SH which is wrong.)

(examples: ICH, RECHT, DURCH, etc.)

B — CH after A, O and U is gutteral (throaty), like the Scottish word LOCH and is pronounced as follows:—

1 — With the BACK of the tongue, lightly touch the BACK of the throat.
2 — Aim a stream of air against the back of the throat.
3 — The escaping air should be heard.
(examples: LACHEN, NOCH, BUCH, etc.)

Final G preceded by I is pronounced like soft CH in some districts of Germany.
(example: WENIG = VEY-NICH; mostly sung this way.)

In other German speaking areas, final G is pronounced as written.
(example: WENIG = VEY-NIG)

Final D is always pronounced hard — like T.
(example: WAND = VAHNT)

Spanish

Spanish	*English*

VOWELS

A . . . . AH (as in FATHER)

E . . . . short EY (as in THEY)

I . . . . EE (as in MEET)

O . . . . short AW (as in SHORT)

U . . . . long OO (as in FOOD)

CONSONANTS

C (in Latin America) . . . . hard S (as in SISTER)

C (in Spain) . . . . hard TH (as in THING)

C (before A, O and U) . . . . K

CH . . . . CH (as in CHESS)

B is SOFT and must be pronounced with very relaxed lips so that it sounds almost, but not quite, like V.
    (example: BEBER = BVAY-BVAYR)

D is also very SOFT and sounds almost, but not quite, like soft TH. (In English D the tip of the tongue flicks the gum just behind the upper front teeth. But in Spanish D the tip of the tongue softly touches the back of the upper front teeth. This is called the DENTAL D.)
    (example: AMAD = AH-MAHDTH, IDO = EE-DTHAW)

J . . . . H (as in HOPE)
    (example: JOSÉ = HAW-SAY)

G (followed by E or I) . . . . gutteral CH (like Scottish LOCH)
    (examples: GENTE = CHEYN-TAY, GIGANTE = CHEE-GAHN-TAY)

GU (followed by E or I) . . . . hard G (as in GO)
    (examples: GUI = GHEE, GUE = GHAY. The U is silent.)
        (Consult the dictionary for rare exceptions)

LL (before a vowel, in Latin America) . . . . . Y
    (examples ESTRELLITA = ESTREY-YEE-TAH)

LL (before a vowel, in Spain) . . . . LY
    (example: ESTRELLITA = ESTREL-YEE-TAH)

                In Latin America: LLORANDO = YAW-RAHN-DAW
                In Spain: LLORANDO = LYAW-RAHN-DAW

Ñ . . . . NY
    (example: CAÑON = KAHN-YAWN)

R . . . . soft R (as in English)

RR . . . . hard R (trilled as in Italian)

S . . . . S (as in SISTER)

QU . . . . K
    (examples: QUE = KAY, QUI = KEE. The U is silent.)
        (Consult the dictionary for rare exceptions)

X (at the end of a word) . . . . KS (as in English)

X (at the beginning of a word) . . . . H (like Spanish J)

X (before a consonant) . . . . S
    (example: EXTRANJERO = ES-TRAHN-HAY-RAW)

Z (in Latin America) . . . . hard S

Z (in Spain) . . . . hard TH (as in THING)
    (example: ZARZUELA = THAHR-THOO-EY-LAH)

General Rules of Spanish Pronunciation: Words ending in a consonant have the LAST syllable accented. Words ending in a vowel have the NEXT-TO-THE-LAST syllable accented. In exceptions, an accent mark is used.

Glossary of Musical Terms

Musical notation cannot possibly show expressions of style, that is, tonal colors. For that purpose certain terms are used. These terms are usually in Italian because music, as we know it today, began in Italy about four centuries ago. Many of those terms have special signs or abbreviations and these are shown in parentheses. The following terms are those most often used for vocal compositions. (The student is advised to obtain one of the many inexpensive paper bound dictionaries of musical terms.)

GENERAL TERMS

AD LIBITUM (ad lib)	At liberty; as you please
COLLA VOCE	The accompanist waits for the singer in an ad lib phrase
DA CAPO (D.C.)	Return to the beginning and repeat
DAL SEGNO (D.S.)	Return to the sign (𝄋) and repeat
FERMATA (⌢) also TENUTO (ten.)	Hold the note longer than written
FINE	The end
POCO A POCO	Little by little; gradually
SENZA	Without
SIMILE (sim)	Similarly; the same

TERMS OF DYNAMICS

CRESCENDO (cresc <)	Gradually get louder
DIMINUENDO (dim >)	Gradually get softer
FORTE (f)	Loud
FORTISSIMO (ff)	Very loud
MESSA DI VOCE (<>)	Start soft, get loud, then soft
MEZZO FORTE (mf)	Medium loud
MEZZO PIANO (mp)	Medium soft
MEZZO VOCE	Half voice; soft
MORENDO also PERDENDO	Dying away
PIANO (p)	Soft
PIANISSIMO (pp)	Very soft
SFORZANDO (sfz)	Very hard accent

TERMS OF TEMPO AND RHYTHM

ACCELERANDO (accel)	Gradually speed up
ADAGIO	Very slow
ALLA BREVE (¢)	Cut-time; half-note gets the beat
ALLEGRETTO	Medium fast
ALLEGRO	Fast
ANDANTE	Moderately slow
A TEMPO	In the original time
LARGHETTO	Fairly slow and broad
LARGO	Very slow and broad
LENTO	Slow
MODERATO (mod)	Medium speed
PRESTO	Very fast
RALLENTANDO (rall)	Gradually slower
RITARDANDO (rit) also RITENUTO (rit)	Gradually slower
TEMPO PRIMO (I°)	Return to original speed
VIVACE (viv)	Lively

TERMS OF EXPRESSION

ANIMATO	Lively; with animation
CANTABILE	In a gentle, smooth manner
DOLCE	Gently
ESPRESSIVO (esp)	With feeling
GIOCOSO	Gaily; playfully
GRAZIOSO	Gracefully
LAMENTOSO	Sorrowfully
LEGATO	The tones connected smoothly
MAESTOSO	Majestically
MISTERIOSO	Mysteriously
PASSIONATO	With fire; passionately
PORTAMENTO	Slide between two notes
RUBATO	Slowing down some notes and speeding up others to make up the lost time
STACCATO	The tones short, disconnected
TRISTE	Sadly

Songs for Baritones and Basses

We assume that most teachers and students are acquainted with the traditional concert repertoire — those great songs which have formed the bulk of concert programs for many generations. These songs must still form the foundation of any good singer's repertoire. But nowadays such songs may be sung to the exclusion of all else only by a voice of such unusual beauty that it absorbs the attention of the listener to the point where he becomes unaware of the program itself. But this is rare and critics (and even regular concert-goers) are grateful not to encounter the usual three or four old Italian songs and the regular group of Schubert songs from Volume I of that master's works. Stereotyped programs have become a bore and for that reason we suggest the following vocal compositions. They are not only beautiful but have the added merit of being unhackneyed. In short, the student is advised to choose (with the help of the teacher) fresh material to balance the traditional songs and thus to make his or her programs as interesting as possible to the audience. (Most songs appear in several Keys. Choose the appropriate Key for your voice.) It must be realized that this brief list is meant only to help the student *start* the adventure of discovering fresh vocal works.

Russian

(Russian songs are sung mainly in English)

ARENSKY	Revery
	The Eagle
BALAKIREFF	O Come To Me
	Young and Bold Am I
BORODIN	Flowers of Love
	Song of the Dark Forest
GRETCHANINOFF	On the Steppe
	The Skylark
MOUSSORGSKY	Hopak
	Trepak
	Cradle Song of the Poor
	The Siege of Kazan (Basses)
RACHMANINOFF	The Lord Is Risen
	O Thou Billowy Harvest Field
	Wie Mir's Weh Thut

French

CHAUSSON	Chanson de Clown
	Serre Chaude
	Apaisement
FAURÉ	Arpège
	Prison
HOLMÈS	Au Pays
MILHAUD	Quatre Poèmes de Léo Larti

German

SCHUBERT	Des Sängers Habe
	Abendröthe
	Der Zürnende Barde
	Freiwilliges Versinken
SCHUMANN	Lieb Liebchen
	Der Kontrabandist
	Belsatzar
BRAHMS	Schwermut (op. 58)
	In der Gasse (op. 58)
WOLF (Hugo)	Bitterolf
	Anakreon's Grabe
STRAUSS (Richard)	Traum Durch Die Dämmerung
	Liebeshymnus
WOLFF (Erich)	Ich Fürcht' Nit Gespenster
	Alle Dinge Haben Sprache

English

We are not listing English-language songs because every well-equipped music shop carries a special folder of the latest, as well as the traditional, American and English vocal works.

Recordings of Great Singers

It is of invaluable benefit to the student to listen to great singers. Frequent attendance at vocal recitals and opera performances is a "must", so the student can both see and hear the finest in beautiful tone, diction, style and stage deportment. Since it is not difficult to see and hear modern singers, the following list of recordings emphasizes the great artists of the past. This list is just an indication of the great vocal treasures available to the modern student.

Coloratura Sop.	ERAT-11	(Victor)	Amelita Galli-Curci
	ML-2084	(Columbia)	Lily Pons
Lyric Sop.	ERAT-21	(Victor)	Elisabeth Rethberg
	LCT-1126	(Victor)	Elizabeth Schumann
	LCT-1133	(Victor)	Maggie Teyte
	7001	(Classic Ed.)	Emmy Destinn
Dramatic Sop.	ERAT-19	(Victor)	Rosa Ponselle
	LRM-7031	(Victor)	Helen Traubel
	EHA-18	(Victor)	Kirsten Flagstad
	LM-1737	(Victor)	Kirsten Flagstad
Mezzo (Sop.)	LM-1793	(Victor)	Gladys Swarthout
	9533	(Decca)	Conchita Supervia
Contralto (Alto)	LM-1146	(Victor)	Marian Anderson
	LM-7008	(Victor)	Marian Anderson
	LCT-1111	(Victor)	Marian Anderson
	149-6	(Remington)	Karin Branzell
	LCT-1005	(Victor)	Schumann-Heink
Lyric Ten.	ERAT-12	(Victor)	Beniamino Gigli
	ERAT-22	(Victor)	Tito Schipa
	ERAT-17	(Victor)	John McCormack
Spinto Ten.	LM-1771	(Victor)	Jussi Bjoerling
Dramatic Ten.	ERAT-5	(Victor)	Enrico Caruso
	ERAT-7	(Victor)	Enrico Caruso
Heldentenor	LCT-1105	(Victor)	Lauritz Melchior
	E-109	(MGM)	Lauritz Melchior
Lyric Bar.	ERAT-25	(Victor)	John Charles Thomas
	7505	(Decca)	Giuseppe De Luca
	451 & 462	(Eterna)	Mattia Battistini
Dramatic Bar.	ERAT-23	(Victor)	Lawrence Tibbett
	474	(Eterna)	4 Wagnerian baritones (Schwarz, Bohnen, Rhode, Zador)
Bass-Baritone	460	(Eterna)	Michael Bohnen
	50019	(Cetra)	Italo Tajo
Basso	LM-1751	(Victor)	Ezio Pinza
	LCT-3	(Victor)	Feodor Chaliapin
	LCT-1157	(Victor)	Alexander Kipnis
Basso-Profundo	199-73	(Remington)	Emanuel List
Many great stars of the past	LCT-1004	(Victor)	Golden Duets
	LCT-1006	(Victor)	Golden Age at the Metropolitan
	LCT-1115	(Victor)	Critic's Choice